MW00387787

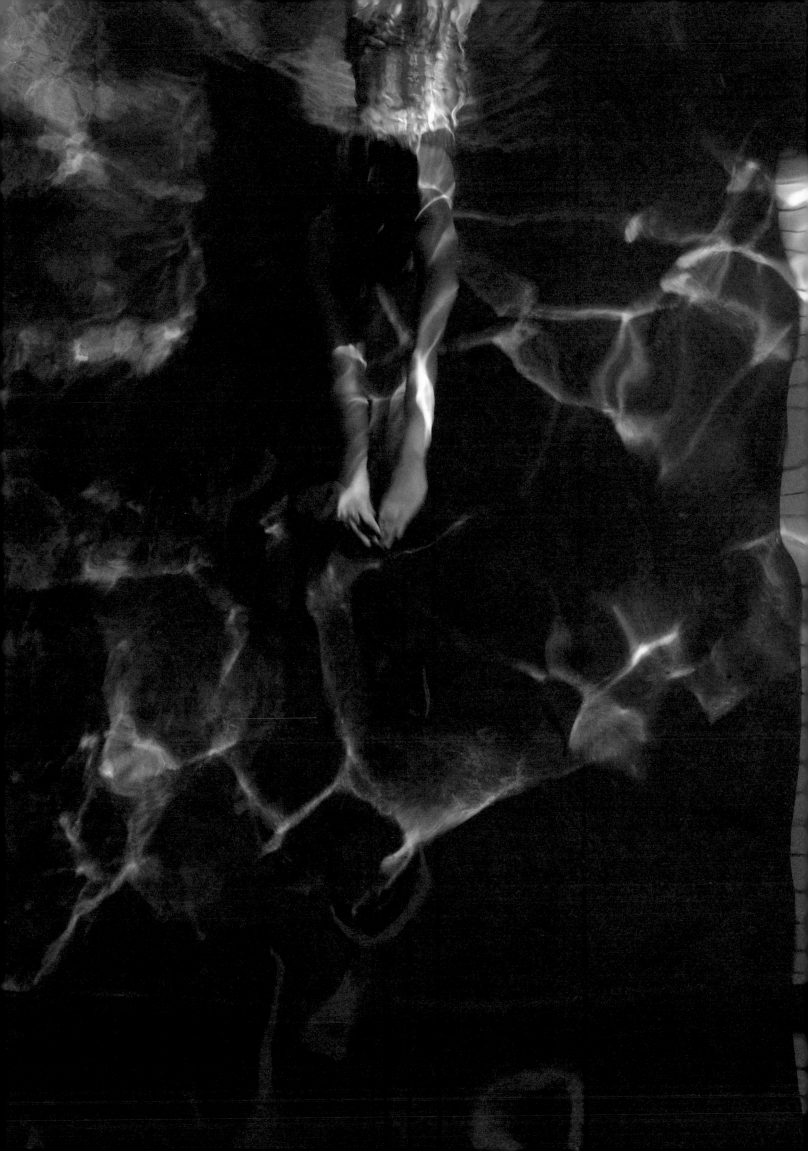

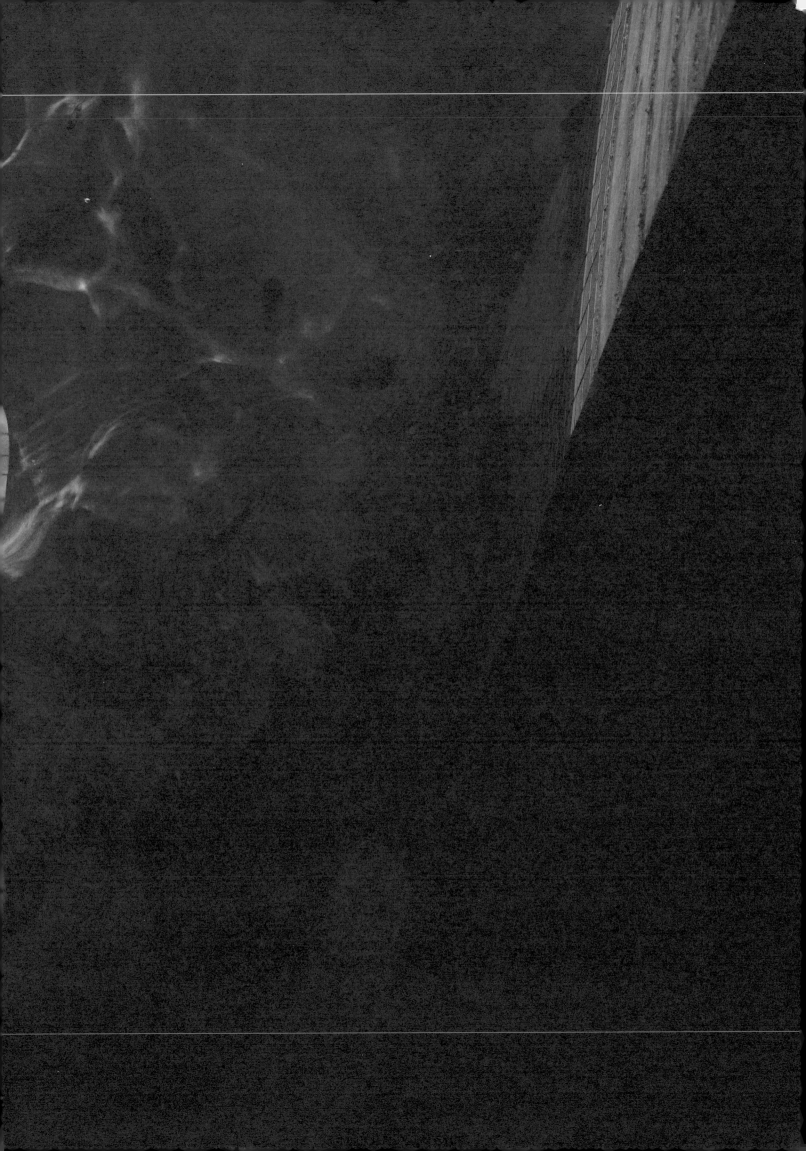

Morphosis: The Crawford House

Overlap

Morphosis: The Crawford House

photographs by Kim Zwarts
essay by Patricia C. Phillips

RIZZOLI
NEW YORK

Project Credits

Morphosis Principals
Thom Mayne
Michael Rotondi

Principal in Charge
Thom Mayne

Project Architects
Kiyokazu Arai
Robin Donaldson

Project Team
Craig Burdick
Martin Mervel
Maya Shimoguchi

Assistants
Birgit Compans
John Enright
David Guthrie
Patrick Hurpin
Tom Lasley
Richard Lundquist
Jason MacDonald-Hall
Tom Marble
Mehran Mashayehk
Jun-ya Nakatsugawa
Katie Phillips
Michael Sant
Selwyn Ting
Remko Van Buren
Dukho Yeon
Ann Zollinger

First published in the United States of America in 1998 by
Rizzoli International Publications, Inc.
300 Park Avenue South, New York NY 10010

Library of Congress Cataloging-in-Publication Data
Morphosis: the Crawford House / photographs by Kim Zwarts ; essay by
    Patricia C. Phillips.
        p.   cm.
    ISBN 0-8478-2082-3 (pbk.)
    1. Crawford House (Montecito, Calif.) 2. Architecture, Postmodern—
California—Montecito. 3. Montecito (Calif.)—Buildings, structures, etc.
4. Morphosis Architects. I. Zwarts, Kim. II. Phillips, Patricia (Patricia C.)
III. Morphosis Architects.
NA7238.M58M67 1998   97-16400
728'.372'0979491—dc21   CIP

Designed by Lorraine Wild
Assisted by Ninotchka Regets and Jody Zellen
Printed and bound in The Netherlands

When Art Is at Home

PATRICIA C. PHILLIPS

The house has to please **everyone,** contrary to the **work of art,** which does **not.** The work of **art is a** private matter for the artist. The house is **not.** The work of art is brought into the world without there being a **need** for it. The house satisfies a **requirement.** The work of art is responsible to **none;** the house is responsible to **everyone.** The work of art wants to draw people out of their state of comfort. The house has to serve comfort....Thus he **loves the house and hates art.** ADOLF LOOS, "ARCHITECTURE," 1910

In his passionate and disputable treatise on the distinctions between art, architecture, and the applied arts, Adolf Loos's simple epigram—"he loves the house and hates art" —remains a reliable catalyst for discussion. Both directly and implicitly the passage quoted above reveals essential tensions inherent in architecture. What are these issues that incite such fierce passions? What is a house and who is it for: the client, the community, the critic? How do Loos's hyperbolic early-twentieth-century observations continue to be relevant at the close of the millennium? Clearly, the past eight decades have provided problematic, even contra-

dictory evidence of houses that have aspired to and achieved the status of art. If function no longer disqualifies a building—the house—as art, how does it affect its aesthetic dimension? The house is an enduring yet restive typology. Like all building types, it is invariably mediated by changing concepts of family, work, sexuality, and habitation. Because it is such a concentrated, contested site of norms and idiosyncracies, it is a seductive if irascible subject for a critic.

This uncompromising dialectic between function and art has been undermined by many other observations and theories that propose more nuanced meanings of house and

home, exposing the house as a site with the supple physical and emotional dimensions informed by cultural standards and individual desires. Current configurations of domesticity accommodate a diversity of lifestyles and issues that places in question any essentialist idea of home, housing, and human experience. As Beatriz Colomina

writes in "Domesticity at War" (OTTAGONO, May 1991), "The domestic has always been at war. The battles of the family, the battles of sexuality, the battle for cleanliness, for hygiene…and now the ecological battle.…War takes place without fighting. The battlefield is the domestic interior: the war cabinet." Is it any surprise that some

of us may hate the house—or at very least embrace its often unsettling ambiguities?

In the architectural and ideological skirmishes of the past decades there has been inadequate consideration of the many ways in which occupants intervene in and experience architecture. In many cases, the soundly contested assumption of a universal, idealized user or participant still exists. Yet architecture is always influenced by people's involvement, by their props and passions. Almost a century ago, Loos estranged and then divorced art and function. But it is precisely their cohabitation that produces resonant stories about houses.

How can—and why shouldn't—architecture and architecture criticism accommodate the aesthetics of occupancy as a function of art? Art and architecture criticism share a productive

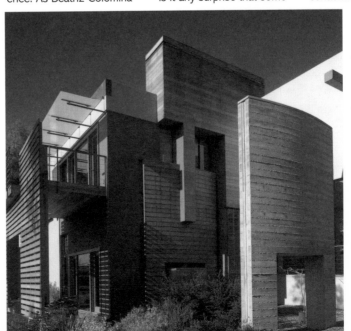

yet inadequately explored territory. The most obvious questions they have in common concern the recipients, not just the producers, of culture. As art continues to explore new paradigms for audience, architecture exposes the complex dimensions of habitation and occupancy. If there were an understanding of when and where art occurs, then might there be more compelling and inclusive ideas of what art is? If art occurs when it actively enters our lives rather than as it leaves the artist's head or hand—at reception rather than conception—then the implications for architecture actually invert Loos's old truism. Function is arguably a prerequisite for art.

How does a house in the late twentieth century differ from earlier houses—the house that Loos considered, for instance? Specifically what occurs when the house is conceived and constructed as art—when the dwelling place is the sought-after object of desire? Clearly, there are

many ways that people can live with art. Collectors and their houses are an intriguing, if extreme, example. Sometimes the objects of desire inscribe a protected, poetic domain: spaces of a house are filled obsessively and rooms overflow with art of proven value or personal significance. In other cases the collection is acquired with indifference, as if an intimate, personal investment might depreciate the collector's judgment or the collection's distinction. When the art collected is, in fact, the house, all of the collector's most extreme ideas and desires are embraced—and at worst, embalmed—in the domestic program. The house becomes the site of deep longing and calculated investment: lived-in art.

There are selected examples of houses that are routinely analyzed, widely admired, and occasionally admonished. Peter Eisenman's brilliant, uncompromised, and demanding residential projects (HOUSE X, for example) reject the

accepted comforts of home in order to fulfill the aspirations of art and creative autonomy. These are difficult houses because of their unyielding commitment to aesthetic and ideological systems. They may be loathed, endured, or loved as homes, but they are unquestionably accepted as art.

No less driven by aesthetic convictions, Morphosis's Crawford House is both a complex record of deliberations between architect and client and an evolving theory of building influenced by the contingencies of site. Here is subtle evidence of spirited exchange, struggle, and settled disputes. The idiosyncratic features of the house manifest a contemporary excursion into the challenging territories of architecture, cultural studies, and occupancy.

In the Crawford House the familiar is simultane-

ously honored and disrupted. A typological foundation—the house—is reconfigured by programmatic experimentation. Morphosis has made a remarkable attempt to represent the conflicting factors of topography, building, and ideology on a single site. The contradictory dimensions of the contemporary domestic program are poignantly represented by competing forms. Morphosis has created a house that both the client and the critic can occupy imaginatively.

The relationship between the car and the house has been a significant preoccupation of twentieth-century architecture and planning. The two are conspicuous and sometimes contentious companions. In most cases the automobile is a prelude to the architecture, defining the terms of expectation. Reyner Banham's first visits to Southern California convinced the architecture critic that he must learn to

drive. His serviceable black bicycle was adequate for London, but the automobile was an indispensable instrument of research in Los Angeles. In the twentieth-century, the view through the windshield of a fast-moving car may be our most significant scopic experience. As Banham taught us, here the car is the primary access to the architecture of regional ecologies.

Driving north from Los Angeles and Santa Monica, U.S. Highway 1 follows a narrow ledge along the Pacific coast. It is a tightrope that forms a dramatic cleft between the ocean's magnificent horizontal sweep and the steep, sensuous hills that rise to the east. The exits on this north-south corridor are not easy, effortless transitions. The Montecito exit for the Crawford House is no exception; it is a wrenching turn. The roads that lead to the house wander through residential neighborhoods of large, often pretentious homes that rest awkwardly on their lots. Occasionally, there is an older, often neglected dwelling that by the grace of age, modesty, or oversight has survived the forces of development.

The visual, sequential approaches to the Crawford House site are metaphors for Morphosis's eloquent negotiation of the obvious and the implicit. The entrance to the main driveway from the west is a generous, gradual introduction to the house and landscape. The driveway is a great arc that sweeps along the side of the hill and crests next to the house on the site's eastern perimeter. The base of the hill affords a panoramic view of the house's rear facade, a stunning, syncopated score of contrasting materials, forms, and tectonic systems. Unlike many villas in which the uninterrupted axial geometry draws the eyes in a single direction, the Crawford House offers a sequence of discontinuous, eccentric views. The west entrance notifies

visitors that this is a contemporary house of skeptical occupation and complex expectations.

Yet there is an alternate route to the house, a public road that winds up the hill parallel to the front of the house on the east side. From this approach, disclosure of the house is suspended. It sits behind a high wall and is accessible only through discreet pedestrian and vehicular portals.

One approach to the Crawford House offers expansive if fragmented points of view; the other frustrates and delays an optical experience. The sweeping arc that inscribes the site suggests expansiveness and access to the home. Paradoxically, the public, "official" entrance is secretive and repressed. The visual treachery suggests that this house has multiple identities. While it securely occupies its site,

it is actually subversive— a misfit in a neighborhood of colonial-inspired estates and Mediterranean knock-offs. It is not unreasonable to imagine the Crawford House in a context that confirms Loos's dated beliefs: a residential community that appears to embrace all of the comforts of home—a place where art is rejected for the pleasures of domestic utility and the mythology of the house as haven.

Morphosis rotates and then fastens this renegade on the edge of the hill. Placed at what would conventionally be the back of the building lot, the Crawford House disrupts commonplace expectations of the country house that rests confidently and centrally on its site. The porous rear, west elevation stretches down from the sloping hillside while the front of the house clenches the crown of the hill. Thick, concrete walls emerge from

the packed cinder driveway. Overlapping planes and volumes anchor the building to its rugged site.

But the reticence of the concealing structures and protective surfaces recedes to reveal an interior that brings people together in a mutual process of investigation. At the entry, a visitor passes through two rough concrete walls that meet to form a passage with a split lintel. Steps rise to an exterior, triangular foyer. In the west corner a rectangular aperture frames a view of a lap pool that extends toward the ocean and is perpendicular to the structural spine of the house. This small room is the symbolic fulcrum of the house. It mediates between the exterior and interior, between general concepts and local contingencies. It is a diminutive site where architecture is concurrently an obstacle and an instigation to explore further. This

transitional space embodies the tension of the domestic program implied by the two approaches to the house.

The Crawford House is based on a series of cartographic strategies that connect abstract and figurative issues, global conventions, and concerns specific to its site. It is a rich, sometimes riotous confederation of symbolic systems that acknowledge the complexities of contemporary life. A tripartite process of mapping first situated the main north-south axis of the house on the Mercator grid. Reference to this invented map projection system that encircles the world and ensnares the imagination connects the Crawford House with other global sites and conditions. Perpendicular to the main axis is the second organizing element, a series of megalithic pylons that hold the site in a tenacious grip. In plan they look like vertebrae, but, like a clenched fist, they evoke energy and

In the Crawford House the familiar is simultaneously **honored and disrupted.** A typological foundation—the house—is reconfigured by **programmatic experiment**ation.

urgency. Clearly, it has been a strenuous feat to secure the house to the land.

There is nothing tempered or tentative about these pylons; they are predominant in plan, elevation, and section. They have a palpable presence. On an initial walk through the house one perceives viscerally and intellectually this spiny procession that both anchors the building and orchestrates spatial and temporal ideas in the interior, which transcends the conventional requirements of bedroom, bathroom, kitchen, and living room. The pylons never undermine the domestic order but rather modulate its impact and importance.

The third structural element is a fragmented, semicircular wall that follows the curved driveway from the west. The wall acknowledges public and private as traditional spatial domains, but it also represents a breakdown of these dialectical conventions; it functions as an idea more than as a tangible, architectonic form. At a time when technology has so radically transformed ideas of public and private, this component clearly questions the function of architecture as a social screen.

Few of us go home to get away from the world.

In fact, it is in the home rather than on the street or at work that the world is most vividly and routinely encountered. The home's heartbeat reverberates with global events. For many, televisions, computers, the Internet, and facsimile machines bring in torrents of information. Privacy is no longer a given in the home; public space may be more of a private enclave.

Traces of this tripartite organizational system throughout the house keep what might have been an unbearable tension of materials, spaces, and details within appreciable limits. Contravening the Mercator grid is a prominent axis created by the triangular entry foyer, the aperture, and the lap pool. Master and guest bedrooms are at the south end; the living room, dining room, and kitchen extend to the north.

There is also a sectional hierarchy. The lower levels of the house contain "summer" spaces; the upper levels, "winter." There are two master bedrooms for the different seasons: at ground level, the summer room is shaded and opens to a patio, the pool, and the surrounding landscape. The floor and other surfaces are resistant and cool. The winter bedroom above is a warm, enclosed space.

It is in the living room where the convergence of systems and structures is most observable. The long room is punctuated by the procession of pylons that pragmatically divide and articulate activity areas as well as accommodate functional elements, including a fireplace and buffet. While the sweep of the semicircular wall outside is not apparent from this room, the vaulted ceiling reiterates its form.

Although the house's front and rear facades present disassociative ideas of domesticity and of the relationship of architecture to site, each has a commanding presence. The extreme modesty of the front entrance stimulates curiosity. Morphosis's

Art was not explored here at an aloof, comfortable distance but deliberately and routinely as part of daily activity. Art prevails when it is susceptible to change, subject to revision, and open to fortuity.

customary palette of unusual if not incompatible materials requires a daring orchestration of tonalities and textures. Here the exterior walls are of cast concrete and their wood-grain surface celebrates the process of production. The triangular vestibule is smooth white stucco; peeking over it are elements clad in copper and wood.

In back, the house presides over the arid landscape. In contrast to the thick compression of volumes and materials at the entrance, the rear facade of stucco surfaces, copper sheathing, concrete and wood plinths, metal and wire railings, and trellises forms an animated, cacophonous collage. Passage through the house from east to west, therefore, reveals its transformation from a protected closure to an exuberant confederation of programmatic ideas and landscape forms.

In plan, two pieces appear to have been cast off the main house. At the north end is a rectangular garage. Behind and beneath it is a studio for the client, a painter. The piece at the south end is more of a fugitive: it appears to have slipped away like a chunk of ice broken off an enormous iceberg; it drifts from the site. This small building is a guest house. Its west facade rises dramatically like the prow of a ship. Behind it, two similar-sized volumes meet to form a "T" that articulates public and private areas. In contrast to the expansive proportions of the main house, the guest house is a crystallization that steps up the steep topography. The spartan scale is rendered in exquisite materials.

Its most curious space is the bathroom—always a favorite room for Morphosis. A room for ablutions, bathing, and sensual activities, the bathroom is one of the most complex spaces in the domestic landscape. Even if appointed graciously, in most houses it is deeply embedded in the most private areas of the building. Here as in many of their projects, Morphosis has created a titillating, voyeuristic space. The entire south wall of the bathroom is glass block that reveals color, movement, light, and activity. Bathing, brushing teeth, and washing hands take place in changing natural light and are suggestively exposed to the outside. This is one of many throughout the

It is a curious process to wander through someone's house, deciphering the conceptual motivations of an architect. As compelling as the generative ideas may be, the lived-in characteristics of the house keep invading and inflecting the theoretical preoccupations. Architecture prevails, but there is a domestic static or interference. One can examine the bold structures and systems that give the house its enduring character; but an article of clothing, cosmetics in the bathroom, books by the bed, a loaf of bread in the kitchen, modulate the authority of theory. Architectural precedents and historical influences intersect with a familial history described by portraits and photographs of birthdays and weddings. All of this evidence of occupancy makes the critical process

a bifocal affair that shifts between the intentions quiet insurrections Crawford House. of theory and the cluttered activities of life. All architecture begins as fiction and ends in reality; criticism begins with reality to discover fiction.

Occupancy embodies the temporal aspect of architecture; its calibrations are the continuing revisions that occur when the architect has retreated and the client has moved in. The house slowly acquires the residue of the residents' desires and improvisations. At first, this transition is a time of tentativeness and tension. The architect's vision is deeply felt; the inevitable pleasures and disarming surprises of possession emerge in a process of habitation. All of the little things that people do to personalize space can seem disrespectful of the architecture. Often these amendments—the objects of family history and habit—are the seeds of an altercation with the

house. Isn't any change potentially perceived as a small demonstration of discontent?

Occupancy is the emergence and inscription of a domestic culture. Supported by the building program, it inevitably challenges, amends, and sometimes skirmishes with the art of architecture. This is a difficult notion for the devoted, conscientious collector to accept. To live one's life may feel like a violation of art, but in order to emotionally and physically inhabit one's own house, the architecture—the art—must somehow be subverted. Occupancy promises to actively reinvent the house so that the equally compelling drives for home and art can coexist.

The Crawford House elicits an appeal for a way to live challenged and comforted by the art that its clients have so devotedly, demonstrably supported and collected. A visit to the house shortly after it was completed revealed evidence of activity and life

in the guest house. Reportedly the clients first used this small building as an office and retreat. There was a productive clutter of papers, books, and furnishings. This little building showed signs of confident occupancy—indications of negotiation between the forceful spaces, formal ideas, and the occupants' desires to make their own home, to find comfort in as well as be challenged by art.

There were understandable reasons why the clients might slip away from the main house to temporarily inhabit this more diminutive building. It is as if the scale of the guest house created a more governable domain. The signs of life do not diminish the aesthetic forces of architecture or the evocative ideas of art. Function informs art; the detritus of human habitation confirms the idea that architecture becomes art at the moment of reception and occupation.

A family's quiet use of a guest house is not something that the commissioned architectural photographer normally documents. Photographs of buildings represent a pre-occupancy condition, a post-occupancy embalming, or some other suspended idea of habitation. In the guest house an engaging sense of unruly occupation had begun to emerge. Art was not explored here at an aloof, comfortable distance but deliberately and routinely as part of daily activity. Art prevails when it is susceptible to change, subject to revision, and open to fortuity. Its poignance is discovered through its alterability.

Most architecture has an immediate audience or an anticipated user. Yet criticism frequently leaves people—and often the client—out of the story and exempt from the critical process. It appears that artists have learned some lessons from architecture's participatory problematics. Architecture is a performative process; its spaces are a prelude to inevitable change and adjustment; and program, more than an account of irritating distractions or expected amenities, is what we believe that we require and desire. These are lessons frequently overlooked by architects themselves, yet it is in these uncontrollable, negotiable, and "performed" aspects of architecture that art resides and flourishes.

The Crawford House is inventive and provocative, and it will change as the occupants fully accept that all buildings have imperfect and inconclusive programs—that art begins when the architect's creation encounters the actual desires and idiosyncracies of the client/audience. This asks for different, perhaps more radical aspirations for architecture—and begs for critical processes that begin to address architecture less as an object and more as performance in which the script is ultimately revised by powerful investigations of improvisation. Morphosis's architectural practice continues to challenge the reliability of many assumptions and singular sources of meaning. Their houses represent the interference of ideas and occupancy. With the Crawford House, Loos's epigram has encountered irrefutable contrary evidence and a persuasive adversary. The transitional conditions of habitation within these provocative spaces enable art to occur, recur—and endure.

Threshold

Threshold

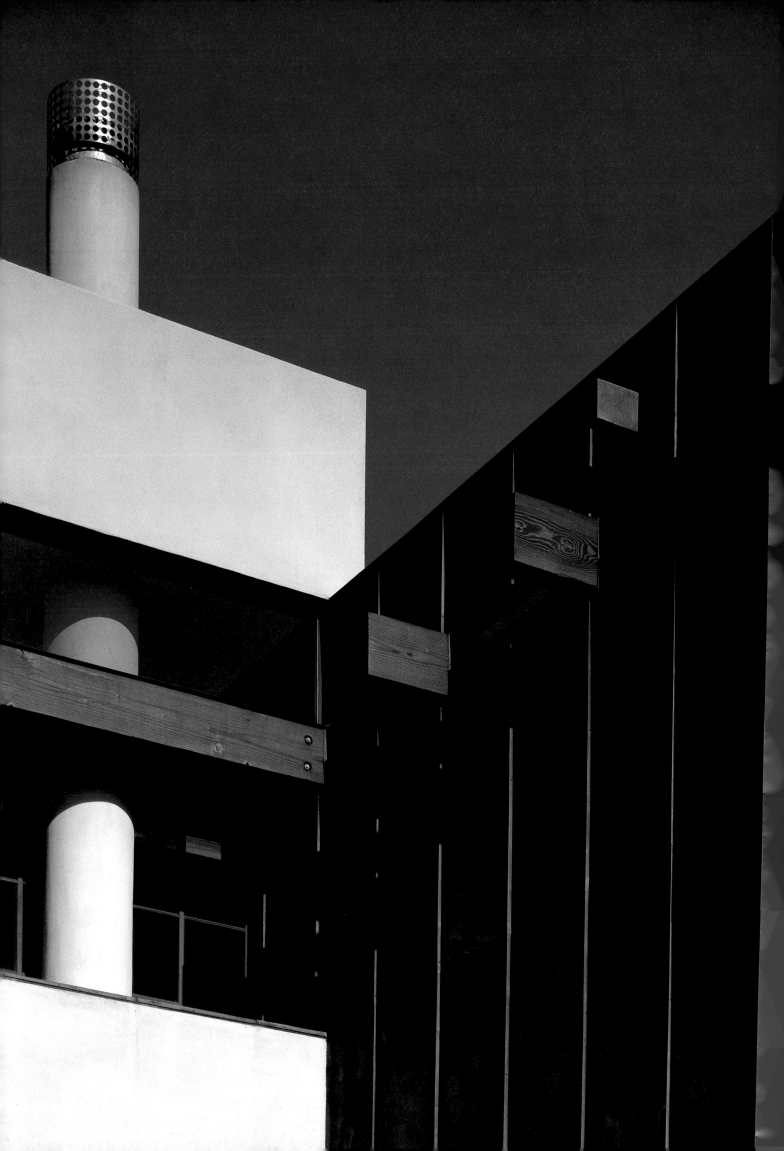

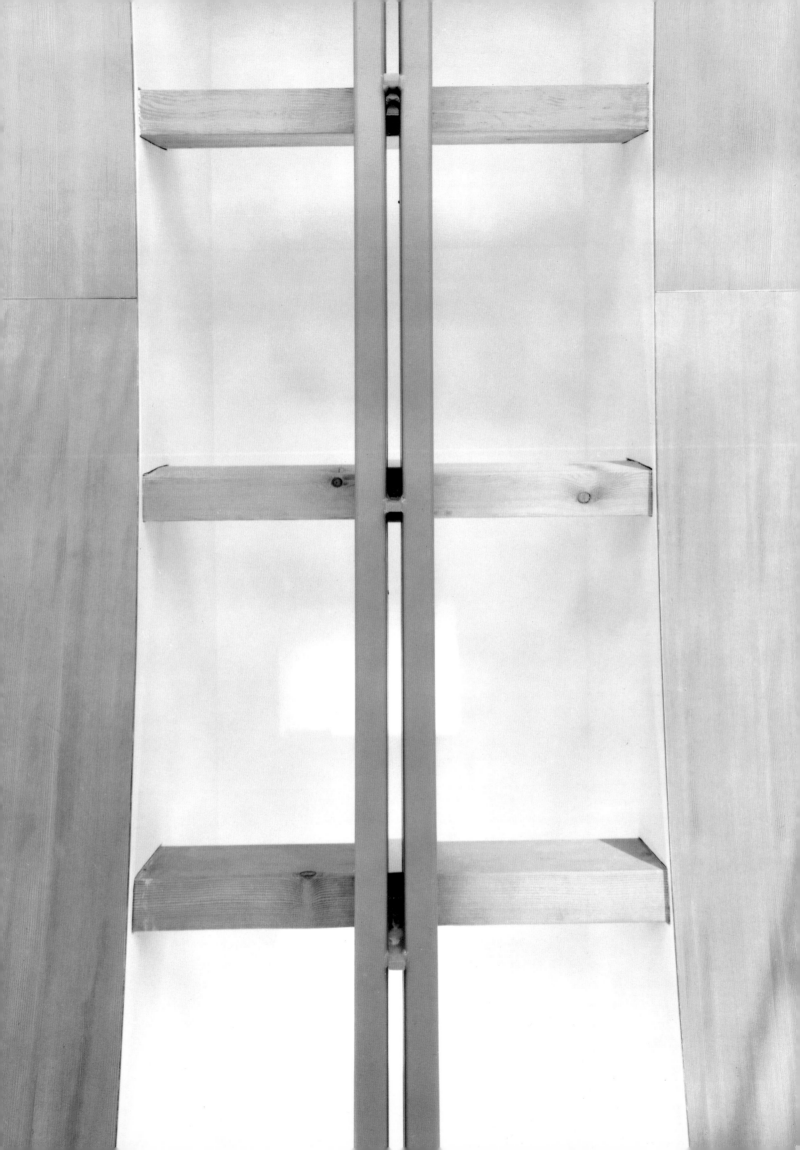

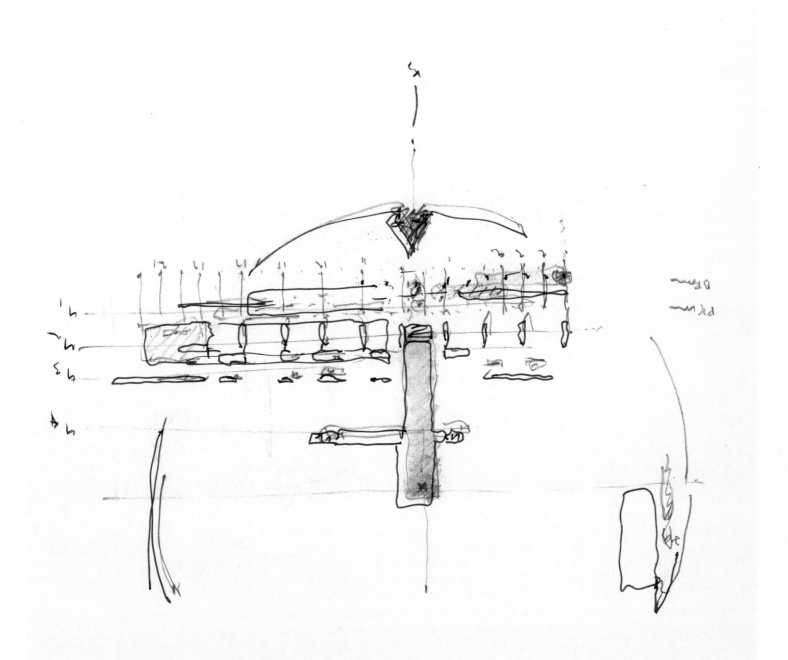

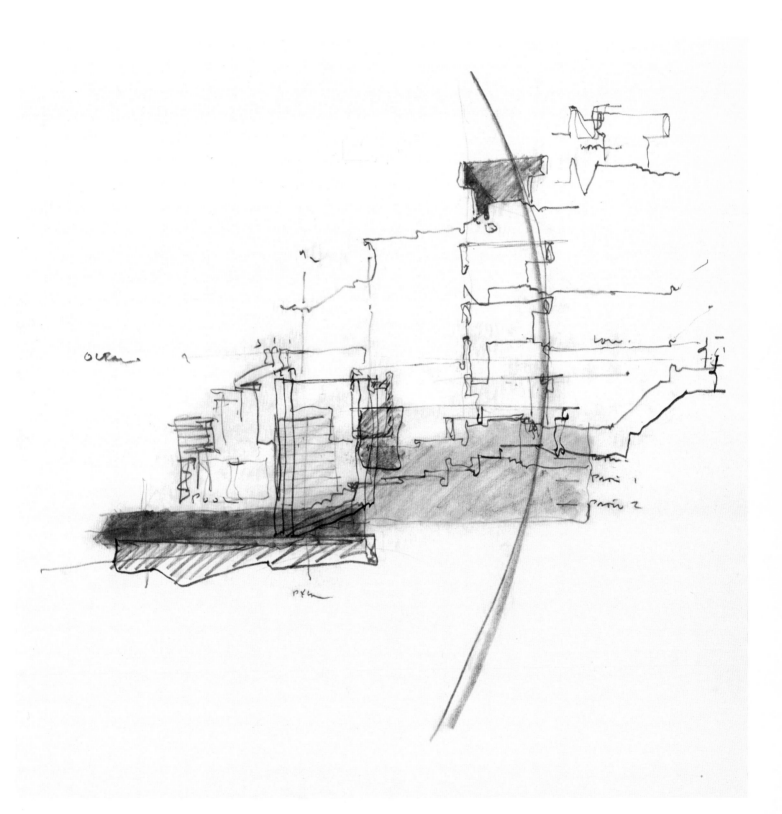

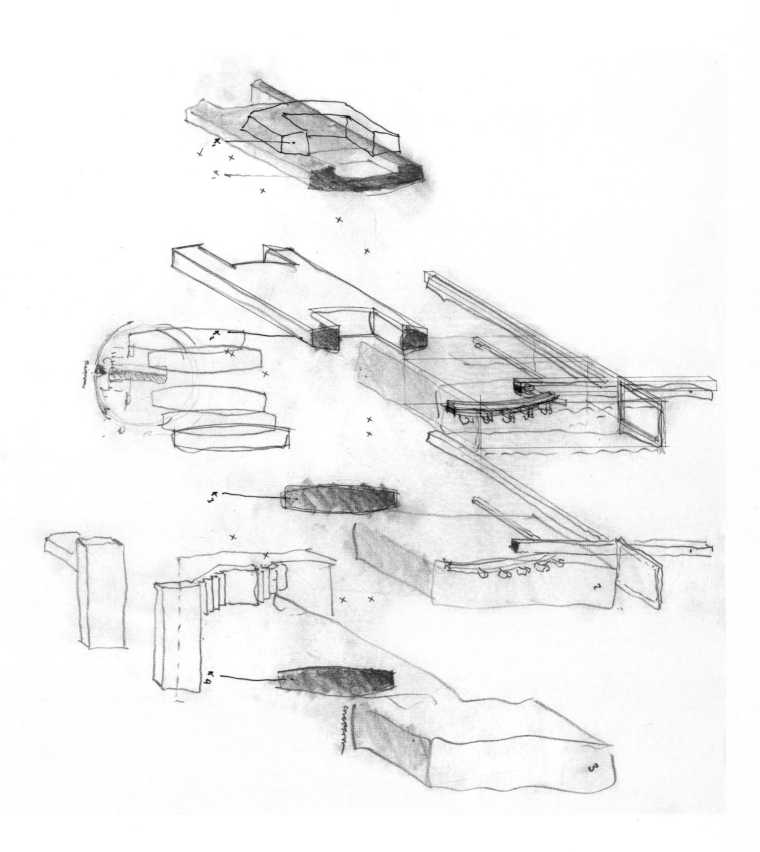

W7 W6 W5 W4 W3 W2 W1 E1 E2 E3 E4

W7 W6 W5 W4 W3 W2 E3 E4

0 16 32

Cadence

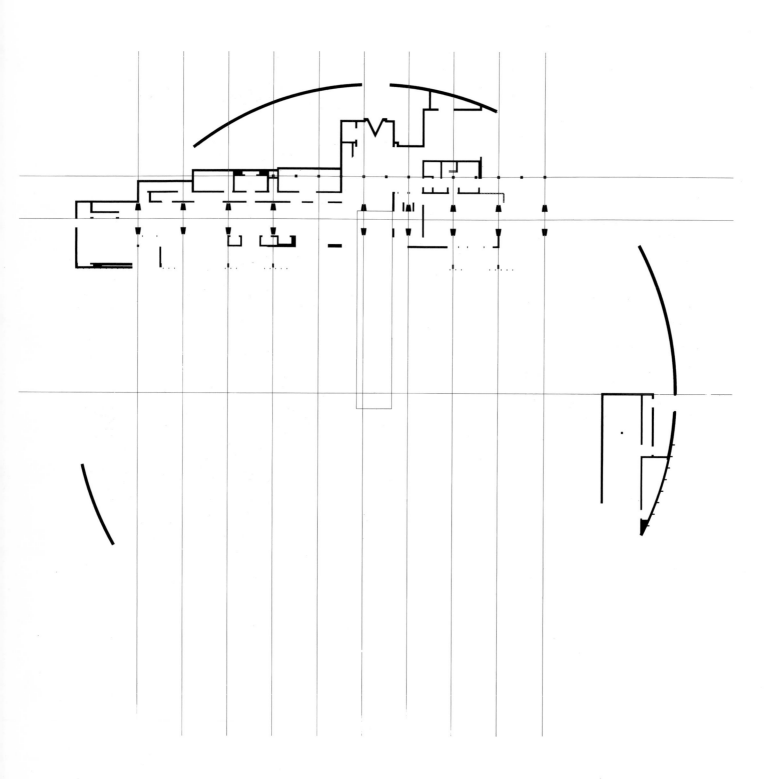

Cadence

parti

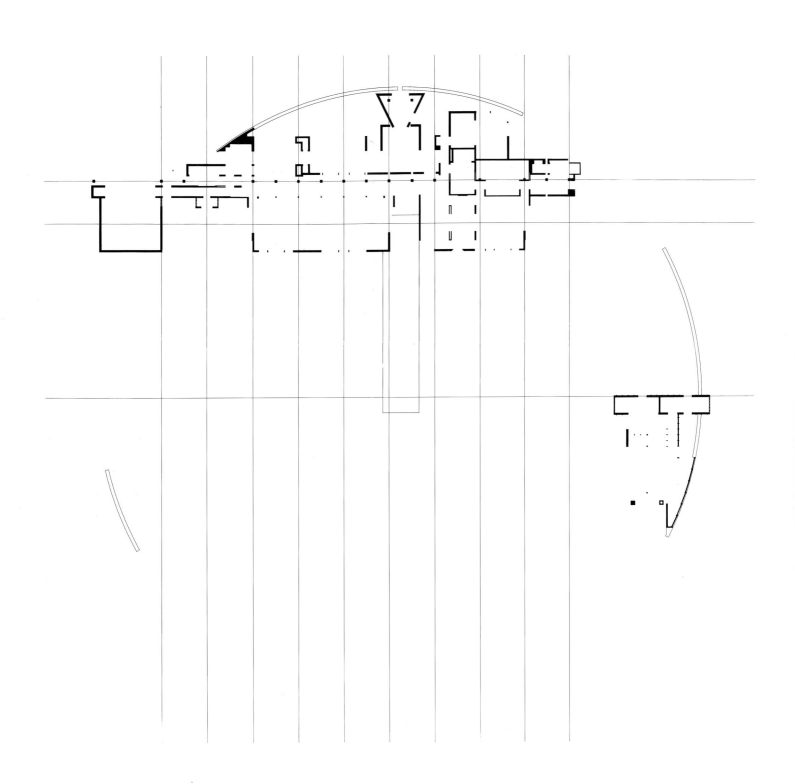

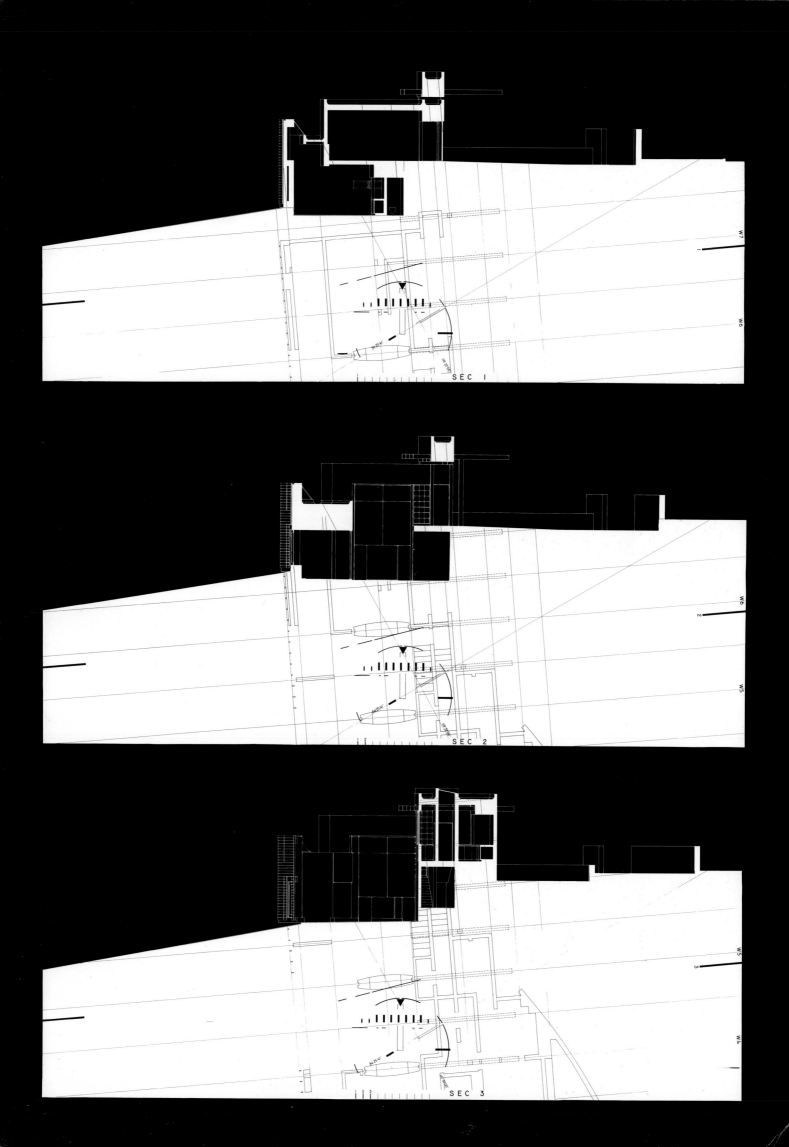

SEC I

SEC 2

SEC 3

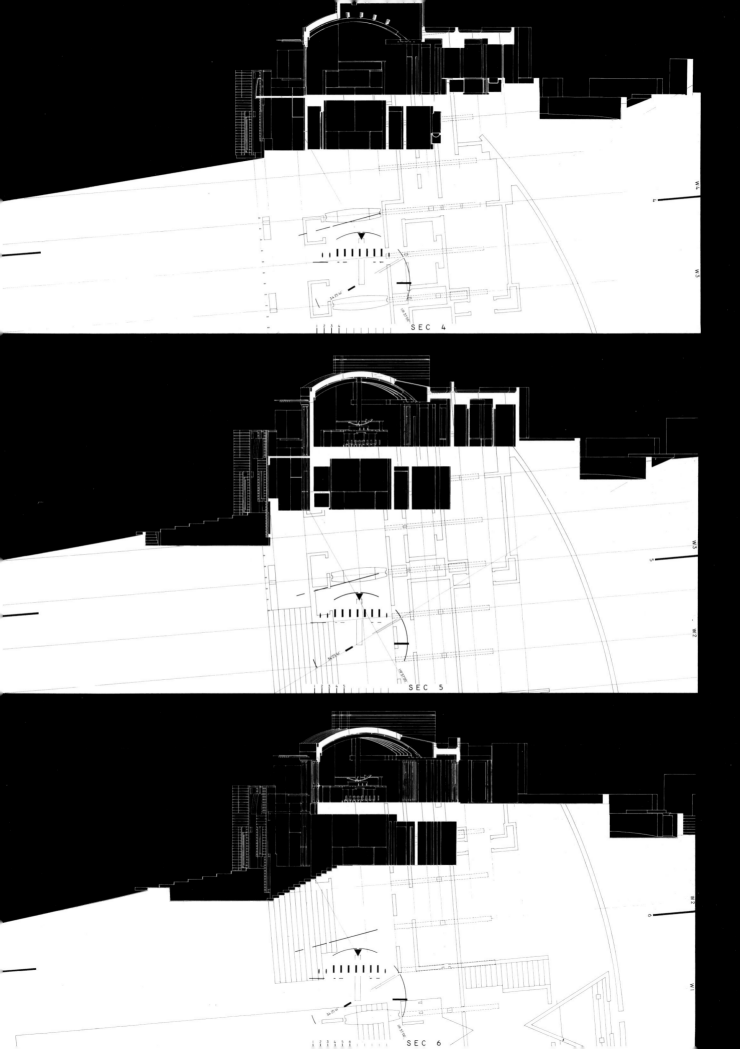

SEC 4

SEC 5

SEC 6

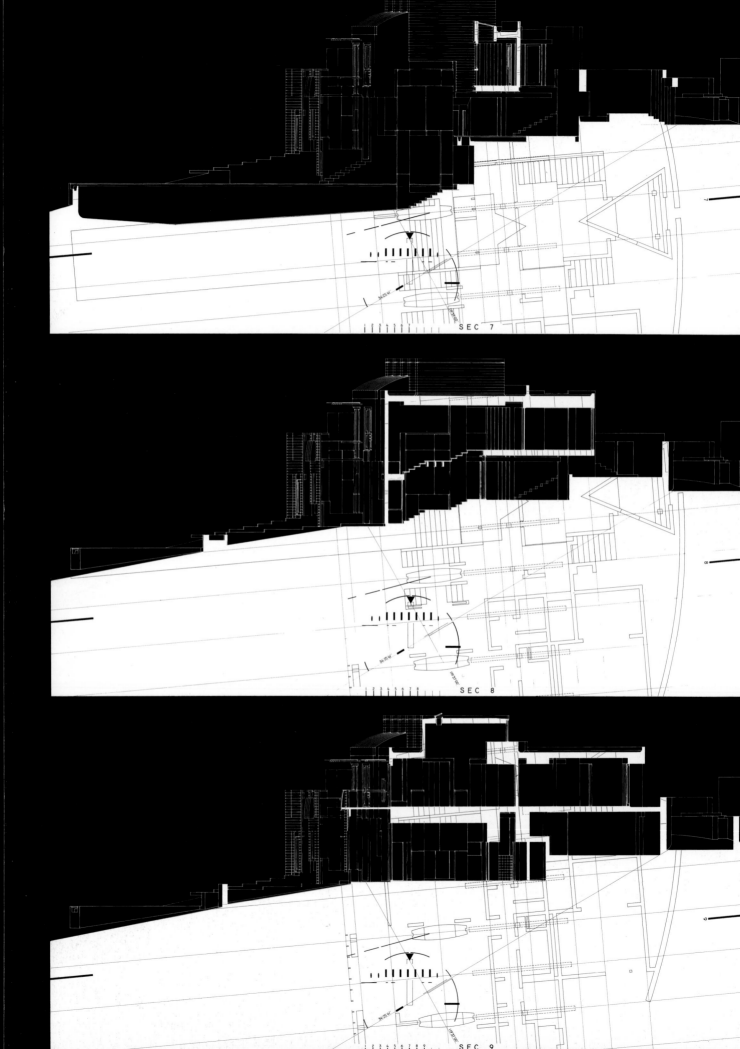

SEC 7

SEC 8

SEC 9

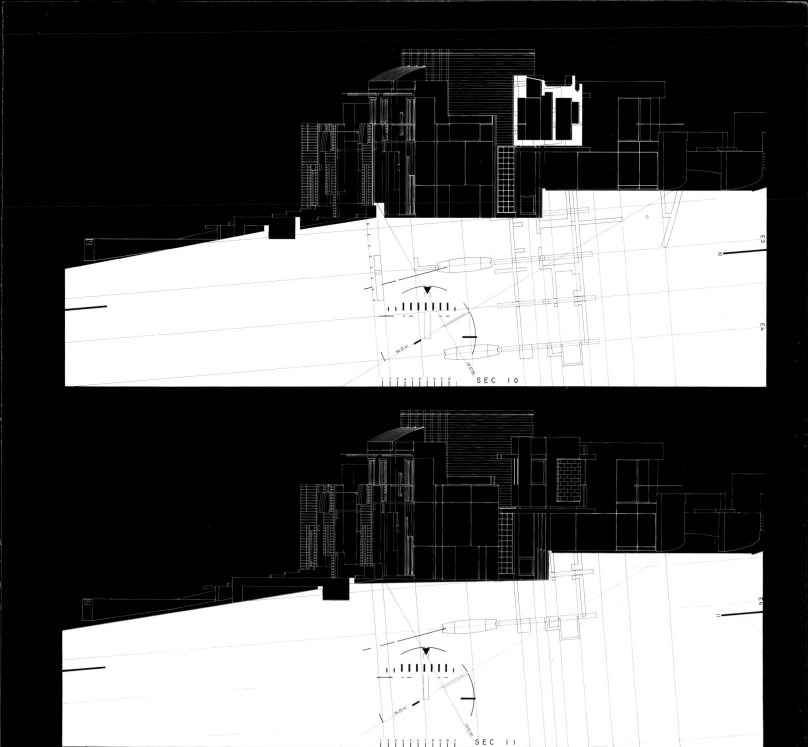

SEC 10

SEC 11

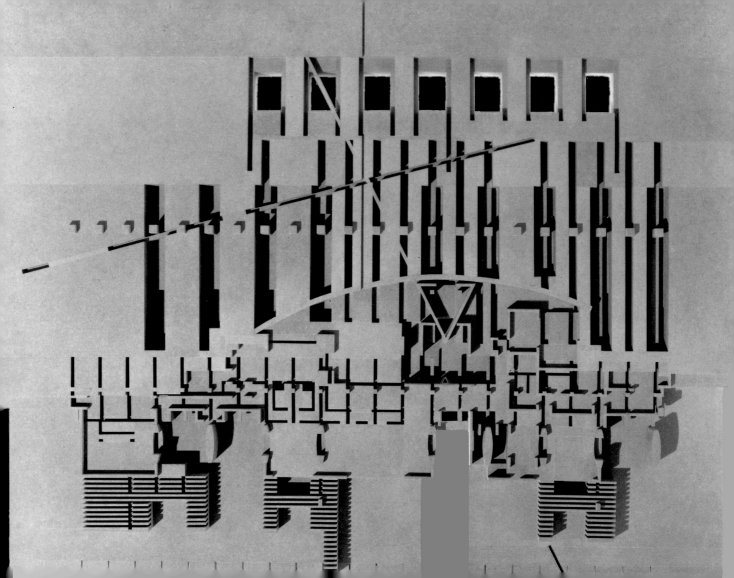

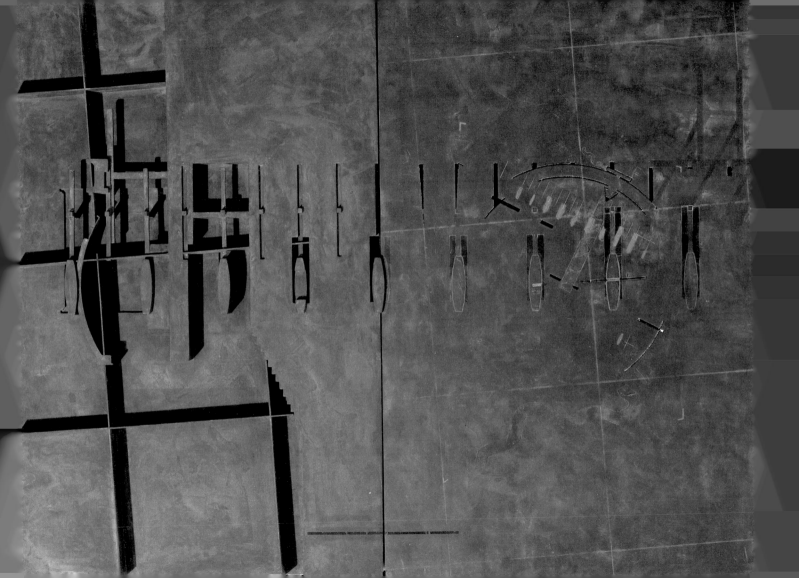

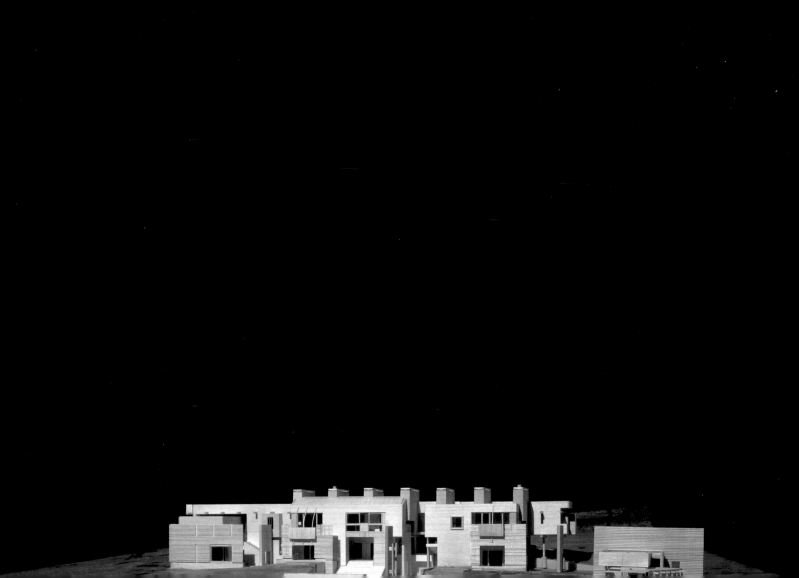

Cadence

The design strategy used in the **Crawford House** initiated a shift from our previous conceptual territory and became the point of departure for a series of later projects. Our current preoccupation with the interrelationship between architecture and landscape continues to evolve in the form of a migration from the suburban to the urban, as the scale of subsequent projects continues to expand. As evidenced in the plan, the Crawford House's primary gesture is a large circular wall. Purposely left unfinished, it defines a new, open-ended project boundary and the initial reference point for occupation of the site. This boundary is disrupted by a system of rhythmic totems and spatial sequences arranged linearly, which transform into topiary walls, fireplaces, stairs, and finally into a purely architectural manifestation of the freestanding concrete pylon. These repetitive elements and

spatial relationships created through a process of excavation, addition, subtraction, and overlay are intended to enhance awareness of movement and exploration as well as promote a haptic experience of the augmented, manipulated landscape field. However, it is the initial gesture of the wall and its relationship to the landscape that most clearly relate to later projects. Through the interplay of built form and the land, the project explores issues of boundary, excavation, movement, and site as a primary element of an architectural language. Through these explorations the Crawford House can be seen as the catalyst of our interest in developing an architectural language that interrogates the dynamic relationship of man and nature.

The architecture fought back but the earth pulled it down, swallowed hard, and chipped a tooth on a bit or wurst.

The Los Angeles **Artspark Competition** (1989) continued our development of an excavating/digging process within the two-hundred acres of a park complex. The horizontal character of the Los Angeles landscape is reiterated by submerging two theaters (one a 2,500 seat proscenium and the other a 500 seat black box) into the ground. This strategy allows the complex to be comprehended as a series of pavilions sited among the smaller-scale

buildings in the park. The public places that are so essential to the theater experience occupy spaces between the horizontal landscape plane and the new subterranean entry. Both automobiles and pedestrians pierce this intermediary zone, with the primary entry consisting of a large stair and ramp descending into the ground, creating a "reverse" *piano nobile*. It is this interstitial space where theater mediates between man and nature.

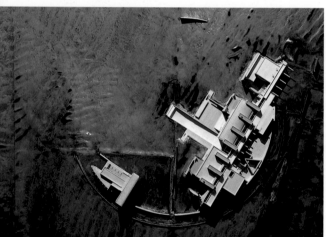

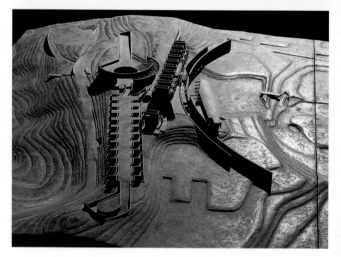

The wall tried to take over the earth.

The earth retaliated and crept over the wall. The wall, humbled, learned its lesson...

The site gesture for the **Chiba Golf Club** (Chiba Prefecture, Japan, 1989–92) began as an immediate departure from the Crawford parti. As the project developed, we increasingly benefited from hindsight as new strategic possibilities emerged. The singular wall of the Crawford House developed into a pairing of walls, which produced an interstitial territory accommodating most of the program. This middle area is

modulated by repetitive light monitors that produce a system of rhythm and movement. The spaces are submerged and subtractive in nature and no longer define an object or iconography of building, but only spaces in-between. The restaurant pavilion explores a more idiosyncratic language that reinterprets the landscape as a fragment of an earth form, and the pavilion acts as a counterpoint to the background elements of the complex.

...and while no one was watching, the earth took over the architecture.

Vienna Expo/ Paris et Utopie

(competitions, 1989 and 1995) further explored the idea of the reconstituted ground plane, but within an increasingly expanded urban scale. Both projects deploy a sectionally generated land form in the shape of a broad curved surface that forms a new ground datum. This surface interacts with various programmatic elements above and below it to produce a series of spaces and objects that interact and develop as a self-generative process. What begins to emerge is not only a new urban landscape that is mimetic of the city's complexity, density, and diversity, but also accidental encounters that form the basis of our program for the contemporary metropolis.

The **Yuzen Vintage Car Museum** (Los Angeles, California, 1991) uses the initial ideas of the Vienna Expo and Paris et Utopie projects to solve a specific urban problem. A new ground plane forms an elevated urban piazza that mediates between two distinct areas of the city. The plane emerges from the earth near the more residential and low-density areas to the south. The roof plane rises to the north, defining the more urban and dense street edge. The form contains programmatic elements—"object buildings"—that articulate scale.

The earth regurgitated and belched, fragments of chaparral scarred its back.

Architecture's last stand, it fled from the earth and emerged with entrails of roses.

The **Science Museum School** (Los Angeles, California, 1991) developed in relation to a Beaux-Arts garden and the three adjacent museum buildings. The school is shrouded by a new land surface used as a connecting device, a linkage, between building and landscape. This surface, reinterpreted from the existing site geometry, incorporates both interior and exterior programmatic spaces. Its expression is intentionally demonstrative, as part of an overall educational strategy.

A residential project whose typology is similar to that of the Crawford House yet less ambitious in scope, the **Blades House** (Santa Barbara, California, 1995) is a direct critique of the Crawford House. The circular wall yields to the site conditions and becomes elliptical, defining an interior/exterior place and demarcating a point of reference for the future work. The spaces inscribed by the wall and the structure piercing through it constitute a less formal, more idiosyncratic organization. Whereas the Crawford House is finally perceived as a collection of elements, the Blades House places more emphasis on the clarity of a singular central space.

The **Hypobank** project (Klagefurt, Austria, 1996–98) synthesizes many of the issues that were first addressed in the Crawford House, beginning with the impulse to "shape" the site as a primary condition. A one-mile-diameter spherical surface penetrates the land, "morphing" into a shallow berm—a three-dimensional manifestation of the agricultural fields on the outskirts of Klagenfurt. Parallel to our investigations in Vienna and Paris, this project is an interplay between the earth form and the found (or proposed) urban fabric of building and infrastructure. A dialogue is generated between these organizational elements, providing complexity, versatility, and visual richness to the diverse demands of the project.

The earth stretched and extended as the battleground grew while small scattered eruptions continue...

JOHN ENRIGHT

I wish to acknowledge Bill and Joan Crawford for entrusting me with the design of their home. Among all possible commissions, a house in particular is never solely informed by the architect's vision...there is simply too much risk at close proximity. Bill and Joan managed to tread the very fine line between building a house that would satisfy their needs for comfort and self expression, and at the same time embarking on and participating in a formal exploration of architecture.

The client/architect relationship is unique in that both parties initially embark on a project in blind faith. To complicate things further, the process of conceiving a private house seems to magnify all that is meaningful to the person, couple, or family that will make it their home. The very personal nature of the enterprise demands a level of intimacy between client and architect that is often somewhat premature. In ideal circumstances, the house becomes an artifact which ultimately concretizes all of the nuances and idiosyncrasies of their relationship through the architect's critical distance.

Our dance of creativity, albeit a labor of love, was not without birth pains and angst. What would begin as a benign discussion of a simple (or not so simple) house transformed into a philosophical inquiry permeated with memories, desires, dreams, hopes, and fears. With the possible exception of psychological therapy, there may be no precedent in life for this kind of interaction, a mutual exploration of uncharted territory. Rising to the occasion with Solomon-like judgment, Bill and Joan dealt with myriad decisions throughout the project while simultaneously challenging us to come to the table with solutions that worked for them yet did not adversely impact the architectural aspirations. Through their patronage, the Crawfords have also contributed to their community, opening the eyes of many people who have never had any other opportunity to experience contemporary architecture.

THOM MAYNE